Wedding Guest Book & Memories

Remember your love story. share memories & write them down. Pass them on. Books With Soul® is a trademark brand and Supports all Authors and copywrite. Check out our full line of books amazon.com/author/bookswithsoul
Isbn:978-1-949325-64-5

Everyone has a story...
This is our story.
The Story of Us

Our story began on:

Our love story is my favorite...

Table of contents:

Section One – Guest Book – A record of everyone who shared our day.

Section Two – Our Wedding Day – A record of the day's events & our honeymoon.

Section Three – Our Home – Where we lived, pets & fun memories.

Section Four – Our Family Tree – A record of births & history of our ancestors.

Section Five – Our Anniversaries – A record of the years of marriage and special occasions.

Section Six – Our Vacations & Adventures – Where we explored and visited together.

Sectionn Seven – The Story Of Us – A record of the things we never want to forget.

Wedding Party:
Bride
Groom

Section One

Guest Book

Name of Guest(s):

Email:

Address:

A word of advice for the lucky couple:

Name of Guest(s):

Email:

Address:

A word of advice for the lucky couple:

Name of Guest(s):

Email:

Address:

A word of advice for the lucky couple:

Name of Guest(s):

Email:

Address:

A word of advice for the lucky couple:

Name of Guest(s):

Email:

Address:

A word of advice for the lucky couple:

Name of Guest(s):

Email:

Address:

A word of advice for the lucky couple:

Name of Guest(s):

Email:

Address:

A word of advice for the lucky couple:

Name of Guest(s):

Email:

Address:

A word of advice for the lucky couple:

Name of Guest(s):

Email:

Address:

A word of advice for the lucky couple:

Name of Guest(s):

Email:

Address:

A word of advice for the lucky couple:

Name of Guest(s):

Email:

Address:

A word of advice for the lucky couple:

Name of Guest(s):

Email:

Address:

A word of advice for the lucky couple:

Name of Guest(s):

Email:

Address:

A word of advice for the lucky couple:

Name of Guest(s):

Email:

Address:

A word of advice for the lucky couple:

Name of Guest(s):

Email:

Address:

A word of advice for the lucky couple:

Name of Guest(s):

Email:

Address:

A word of advice for the lucky couple:

Name of Guest(s):

Name of Guest(s):

Email:

Email:

Address:

Address:

A word of advice for the lucky couple:

A word of advice for the lucky couple:

Name of Guest(s):

Email:

Address:

A word of advice for the lucky couple:

Name of Guest(s):

Email:

Address:

A word of advice for the lucky couple:

Name of Guest(s):

Name of Guest(s):

Email:

Email:

Address:

Address:

A word of advice for the lucky couple:

A word of advice for the lucky couple:

Name of Guest(s):

Email:

Address:

A word of advice for the lucky couple:

Name of Guest(s):

Email:

Address:

A word of advice for the lucky couple:

Name of Guest(s):

Email:

Address:

A word of advice for the lucky couple:

Name of Guest(s):

Email:

Address:

A word of advice for the lucky couple:

Name of Guest(s):

Email:

Address:

A word of advice for the lucky couple:

Name of Guest(s):

Email:

Address:

A word of advice for the lucky couple:

Name of Guest(s):

Email:

Address:

A word of advice for the lucky couple:

Name of Guest(s):

Email:

Address:

A word of advice for the lucky couple:

Name of Guest(s):

Email:

Address:

A word of advice for the lucky couple:

Name of Guest(s):

Email:

Address:

A word of advice for the lucky couple:

Name of Guest(s):

Email:

Address:

A word of advice for the lucky couple:

Name of Guest(s):

Email:

Address:

A word of advice for the lucky couple:

Name of Guest(s):

Email:

Address:

A word of advice for the lucky couple:

Name of Guest(s):

Email:

Address:

A word of advice for the lucky couple:

Name of Guest(s):

Email:

Address:

Name of Guest(s):

Email:

Address:

A word of advice for the lucky couple:

A word of advice for the lucky couple:

Name of Guest(s):

Name of Guest(s):

Email:

Email:

Address:

Address:

A word of advice for the lucky couple:

A word of advice for the lucky couple:

Name of Guest(s):

Email:

Address:

A word of advice for the lucky couple:

Name of Guest(s):

Email:

Address:

A word of advice for the lucky couple:

Name of Guest(s):

Email:

Address:

A word of advice for the lucky couple:

Name of Guest(s):

Email:

Address:

A word of advice for the lucky couple:

Name of Guest(s):

Email:

Address:

A word of advice for the lucky couple:

Name of Guest(s):

Email:

Address:

A word of advice for the lucky couple:

Name of Guest(s):

Email:

Address:

A word of advice for the lucky couple:

Name of Guest(s):

Email:

Address:

A word of advice for the lucky couple:

Name of Guest(s):

Name of Guest(s):

Email:

Email:

Address:

Address:

A word of advice for the lucky couple:

A word of advice for the lucky couple:

Name of Guest(s):

Email:

Address:

A word of advice for the lucky couple:

Name of Guest(s):

Email:

Address:

A word of advice for the lucky couple:

Name of Guest(s):

Email:

Address:

A word of advice for the lucky couple:

Name of Guest(s):

Email:

Address:

A word of advice for the lucky couple:

Name of Guest(s):

Name of Guest(s):

Email:

Email:

Address:

Address:

A word of advice for the lucky couple:

A word of advice for the lucky couple:

Name of Guest(s):

Name of Guest(s):

Email:

Email:

Address:

Address:

A word of advice for the lucky couple:

A word of advice for the lucky couple:

Name of Guest(s):

Email:

Address:

A word of advice for the lucky couple:

Name of Guest(s):

Email:

Address:

A word of advice for the lucky couple:

Name of Guest(s):

Email:

Address:

A word of advice for the lucky couple:

Name of Guest(s):

Email:

Address:

A word of advice for the lucky couple:

Name of Guest(s):

Email:

Address:

A word of advice for the lucky couple:

Name of Guest(s):

Email:

Address:

A word of advice for the lucky couple:

Name of Guest(s):

Email:

Address:

A word of advice for the lucky couple:

Name of Guest(s):

Email:

Address:

A word of advice for the lucky couple:

Name of Guest(s):

Email:

Address:

A word of advice for the lucky couple:

Name of Guest(s):

Email:

Address:

A word of advice for the lucky couple:

Name of Guest(s):

Email:

Address:

A word of advice for the lucky couple:

Name of Guest(s):

Email:

Address:

A word of advice for the lucky couple:

Name of Guest(s):

Name of Guest(s):

Email:

Email:

Address:

Address:

A word of advice for the lucky couple:

A word of advice for the lucky couple:

Name of Guest(s):

Email:

Address:

A word of advice for the lucky couple:

Name of Guest(s):

Email:

Address:

A word of advice for the lucky couple:

Name of Guest(s):

Email:

Address:

A word of advice for the lucky couple:

Name of Guest(s):

Email:

Address:

A word of advice for the lucky couple:

Name of Guest(s):

Email:

Address:

A word of advice for the lucky couple:

Name of Guest(s):

Email:

Address:

A word of advice for the lucky couple:

Name of Guest(s):

Name of Guest(s):

Email:

Email:

Address:

Address:

A word of advice for the lucky couple:

A word of advice for the lucky couple:

Name of Guest(s):

Email:

Address:

A word of advice for the lucky couple:

Name of Guest(s):

Email:

Address:

A word of advice for the lucky couple:

Name of Guest(s):

Email:

Address:

A word of advice for the lucky couple:

Name of Guest(s):

Email:

Address:

A word of advice for the lucky couple:

Name of Guest(s):

Email:

Address:

A word of advice for the lucky couple:

Name of Guest(s):

Email:

Address:

A word of advice for the lucky couple:

Name of Guest(s):

Email:

Address:

A word of advice for the lucky couple:

Name of Guest(s):

Email:

Address:

A word of advice for the lucky couple:

Name of Guest(s):

Email:

Address:

A word of advice for the lucky couple:

Name of Guest(s):

Email:

Address:

A word of advice for the lucky couple:

Name of Guest(s):

Email:

Address:

A word of advice for the lucky couple:

Name of Guest(s):

Email:

Address:

A word of advice for the lucky couple:

Name of Guest(s):

Email:

Address:

A word of advice for the lucky couple:

Name of Guest(s):

Email:

Address:

A word of advice for the lucky couple:

Name of Guest(s):

Email:

Address:

Name of Guest(s):

Email:

Address:

A word of advice for the lucky couple:

A word of advice for the lucky couple:

Name of Guest(s):

Email:

Address:

A word of advice for the lucky couple:

Name of Guest(s):

Email:

Address:

A word of advice for the lucky couple:

Name of Guest(s):

Email:

Address:

A word of advice for the lucky couple:

Name of Guest(s):

Email:

Address:

A word of advice for the lucky couple:

Name of Guest(s):

Email:

Address:

A word of advice for the lucky couple:

Name of Guest(s):

Email:

Address:

A word of advice for the lucky couple:

Name of Guest(s):

Email:

Address:

A word of advice for the lucky couple:

Name of Guest(s):

Email:

Address:

A word of advice for the lucky couple:

Name of Guest(s):

Email:

Address:

A word of advice for the lucky couple:

Name of Guest(s):

Email:

Address:

A word of advice for the lucky couple:

Name of Guest(s):

Email:

Address:

A word of advice for the lucky couple:

Name of Guest(s):

Email:

Address:

A word of advice for the lucky couple:

Name of Guest(s):

Email:

Address:

A word of advice for the lucky couple:

Name of Guest(s):

Email:

Address:

A word of advice for the lucky couple:

Name of Guest(s):

Email:

Address:

A word of advice for the lucky couple:

Name of Guest(s):

Email:

Address:

A word of advice for the lucky couple:

Name of Guest(s):

Email:

Address:

A word of advice for the lucky couple:

Name of Guest(s):

Email:

Address:

A word of advice for the lucky couple:

Name of Guest(s):

Email:

Address:

A word of advice for the lucky couple:

Name of Guest(s):

Email:

Address:

A word of advice for the lucky couple:

Name of Guest(s):

Email:

Address:

A word of advice for the lucky couple:

Name of Guest(s):

Email:

Address:

A word of advice for the lucky couple:

Name of Guest(s):

Email:

Address:

A word of advice for the lucky couple:

Name of Guest(s):

Email:

Address:

A word of advice for the lucky couple:

Name of Guest(s):

Email:

Address:

A word of advice for the lucky couple:

Name of Guest(s):

Email:

Address:

A word of advice for the lucky couple:

Name of Guest(s):

Email:

Address:

A word of advice for the lucky couple:

Name of Guest(s):

Email:

Address:

A word of advice for the lucky couple:

Name of Guest(s):

Email:

Address:

A word of advice for the lucky couple:

Name of Guest(s):

Email:

Address:

A word of advice for the lucky couple:

Name of Guest(s):

Email:

Address:

A word of advice for the lucky couple:

Name of Guest(s):

Email:

Address:

A word of advice for the lucky couple:

Name of Guest(s):

Email:

Address:

A word of advice for the lucky couple:

Name of Guest(s):

Email:

Address:

A word of advice for the lucky couple:

Name of Guest(s):

Email:

Address:

A word of advice for the lucky couple:

Name of Guest(s):

Email:

Address:

A word of advice for the lucky couple:

Name of Guest(s):

Email:

Address:

A word of advice for the lucky couple:

Name of Guest(s):

Email:

Address:

A word of advice for the lucky couple:

Name of Guest(s):

Email:

Address:

A word of advice for the lucky couple:

Name of Guest(s):

Email:

Address:

A word of advice for the lucky couple:

Name of Guest(s):

Email:

Address:

A word of advice for the lucky couple:

Name of Guest(s):

Email:

Address:

A word of advice for the lucky couple:

Name of Guest(s):

Email:

Address:

A word of advice for the lucky couple:

Name of Guest(s):

Email:

Address:

A word of advice for the lucky couple:

Name of Guest(s):

Email:

Address:

A word of advice for the lucky couple:

Name of Guest(s):

Email:

Address:

A word of advice for the lucky couple:

Name of Guest(s):

Email:

Address:

A word of advice for the lucky couple:

Name of Guest(s):

Email:

Address:

A word of advice for the lucky couple:

Name of Guest(s):

Email:

Address:

A word of advice for the lucky couple:

Name of Guest(s):

Email:

Address:

A word of advice for the lucky couple:

Name of Guest(s):

Email:

Address:

A word of advice for the lucky couple:

Name of Guest(s):

Email:

Address:

A word of advice for the lucky couple:

Name of Guest(s):

Email:

Address:

A word of advice for the lucky couple:

Name of Guest(s):

Email:

Address:

A word of advice for the lucky couple:

Name of Guest(s):

Email:

Address:

A word of advice for the lucky couple:

Name of Guest(s):

Email:

Address:

A word of advice for the lucky couple:

Name of Guest(s):

Email:

Address:

A word of advice for the lucky couple:

Name of Guest(s):

Email:

Address:

A word of advice for the lucky couple:

Name of Guest(s):

Email:

Address:

A word of advice for the lucky couple:

Name of Guest(s):

Email:

Address:

A word of advice for the lucky couple:

Name of Guest(s):

Email:

Address:

A word of advice for the lucky couple:

Name of Guest(s):

Email:

Address:

A word of advice for the lucky couple:

Name of Guest(s):

Email:

Address:

A word of advice for the lucky couple:

Name of Guest(s):

Email:

Address:

A word of advice for the lucky couple:

Section Two

Our Wedding Day

When you find someone you just know...

Our Wedding Day:

Date:

Locations:

What time it started:

Music? Our song?

What was the weather like?

One of our favorite memories:

I hope I never forget:

Our Wedding:

Food:

The moment I will never forget:

One of our favorite surprises:

One sentence to describe the epic day we became one:

Flowers:

Cake or dessert:

Funny moment :

Wedding Moments:

One of our favorite memories:

Our Wedding Vows:

_____   _____
_____   _____
_____   _____
_____   _____
_____   _____
_____   _____
_____   _____
_____   _____

Our Wedding Vows:

Wedding Moments:

One of our favorite memories:

Wedding Toasts:

Wedding Moments:

One of our favorite memories:

Honeymoon:

Date:

Where we slept:

Locations we visited:

Best or Unique food:

One of our favorite memories:

I hope I never forget:

Honeymoon Memories:

Honeymoon:

Date:

Where we slept:

Locations we visited:

Best or Unique food:

One of our favorite memories:

I hope I never forget:

Honeymoon Memories:

Honeymoon:

Date:

Where we slept:

Locations we visited:

Best or Unique food:

One of our favorite memories:

I hope I never forget:

Honeymoon Memories:

Section Four

Our Home

Where you are is my home...

Our Home:

Address:

_____

How long did we live here:

_____
_____
_____

Favorite features of our place?

One of our favorite memories:
_____
_____
_____
_____
_____

I hope I never forget:

Other Locations where we lived:

Address:

_____

How long did we live here:

_____
_____
_____

Favorite features of our place?

One of our favorite memories:
_____
_____
_____
_____
_____

I hope I never forget:

Our Home:

Address:
_____

How long did we live here:
_____
_____

Favorite features of our place?

One of our favorite memories:
_____
_____
_____
_____

I hope I never forget:

Other Locations where we lived:

Address:

_____

How long did we live here:

_____
_____
_____

Favorite features of our place?

One of our favorite memories:
_____
_____
_____
_____

I hope I never forget:

Other Locations where we lived:

Address:
_____

How long did we live here:
_____
_____

Favorite features of our place?

One of our favorite memories:
_____
_____
_____
_____
_____

I hope I never forget:

Other Locations where we lived:

Address:

_____

How long did we live here:

_____
_____
_____

Favorite features of our place?

One of our favorite memories:
_____
_____
_____
_____
_____

I hope I never forget:

Pets:

Where we found them:

Date they became part of us:

Names and DOB

What did they look like:

One of our favorite memories of our pets:

I hope I never forget:

Moments to Remember:

_____
_____
_____
_____
_____
_____
_____
_____

_____
_____
_____
_____
_____
_____
_____
_____

Pets:

_____

Date they became part of us:

_____

Names and DOB

_____
_____

Where we found them:

_____
_____

What did they look like:

_____
_____

One of our favorite memories of our pets:

I hope I never forget:

_____

Moments to Remember:

_____   _____
_____   _____
_____   _____
_____   _____
_____   _____
_____   _____
_____   _____
_____   _____

All we need is Faith, Hope and Love but the greatest of these is love...

Our Family Tree:

Our Family Tree:

_____ | _____
_____ | _____
_____ | _____
_____ | _____
_____ | _____
_____ | _____
_____ | _____
_____ | _____

Dates of Births and Deaths:

_____
_____
_____
_____
_____
_____
_____

Our Family Tree:

_____ | _____
_____ | _____
_____ | _____
_____ | _____
_____ | _____
_____ | _____
_____ | _____

Dates of Births and Deaths:

_____
_____
_____
_____
_____
_____
_____

Children:

Name:
_____

Weight:
_____

Why we chose their name:
_____
_____

Date of Birth/ Day of Week/Time of Birth:
_____
_____

What did they look like:
_____
_____

One of our favorite memories of this pregnancy and birth:

```
┌─────────────────────────────────────────────┐
│                                             │
│                                             │
│                                             │
│                                             │
└─────────────────────────────────────────────┘
```

I hope I never forget:
_____
_____

Moments to Remember:

Children:

Name:
_____

Weight:
_____

Why we chose their name:
_____
_____
_____

Date of Birth/ Day of Week/Time of Birth:
_____
_____

What did they look like:
_____
_____
_____

One of our favorite memories of this pregnancy and birth:

```
┌─────────────────────────────────────────────────┐
│                                                 │
│                                                 │
│                                                 │
│                                                 │
└─────────────────────────────────────────────────┘
```

I hope I never forget:
_____
_____

Moments to Remember:

_____   _____
_____   _____
_____   _____
_____   _____
_____   _____
_____   _____
_____   _____
_____   _____

Children:

Name:
_____

Weight:
_____

Why we chose their name:
_____
_____
_____

Date of Birth/ Day of Week/Time of Birth:
_____
_____
_____

What did they look like:
_____
_____
_____

One of our favorite memories of this pregnancy and birth:

┌───┐
│   │
│   │
│   │
│   │
└───┘

I hope I never forget:
_____
_____

Moments to Remember:

_____   _____
_____   _____
_____   _____
_____   _____
_____   _____
_____   _____
_____   _____
_____   _____

Children:

Name:
_____

Weight:
_____

Why we chose their name:
_____
_____

Date of Birth / Day of Week / Time of Birth:
_____
_____

What did they look like:
_____
_____

One of our favorite memories of this pregnancy and birth:

```
┌─────────────────────────────────────────────────┐
│                                                 │
│                                                 │
│                                                 │
│                                                 │
└─────────────────────────────────────────────────┘
```

I hope I never forget:
_____
_____

Moments to Remember:

_____

_____

_____

_____

_____

_____

_____

_____

_____

_____

_____

_____

_____

_____

_____

_____

Children:

Name:

Weight:

Why we chose their name:

Date of Birth/ Day of Week/Time of Birth:

What did they look like:

One of our favorite memories of this pregnancy and birth:

I hope I never forget:

Moments to Remember:

_____ _____

_____ _____

_____ _____

_____ _____

_____ _____

_____ _____

_____ _____

_____ _____

Children:

Name:
_____

Weight:
_____

Why we chose their name:
_____
_____
_____

Date of Birth/ Day of Week/Time of Birth:
_____
_____

What did they look like:
_____
_____
_____

One of our favorite memories of this pregnancy and birth:

```
┌─────────────────────────────────────────────────────────┐
│                                                         │
│                                                         │
│                                                         │
│                                                         │
└─────────────────────────────────────────────────────────┘
```

I hope I never forget:
_____
_____

Moments to Remember:

Our Anniversaries

I'll always love you like it was the beginning...

Our Frist Anniversary:

The first year is one epic year, what do we most want to remember about this first year:

Memories of Anniversaries:

I never want to forget:

Five Epic Years:

_____   _____
_____   _____
_____   _____
_____   _____
_____   _____
_____   _____
_____   _____
_____   _____

I never want to forget:

Memories of Anniversaries:

_____
_____
_____
_____
_____
_____
_____
_____

Memories of Anniversaries:

_____
_____
_____
_____
_____
_____
_____
_____
_____

Memories of Anniversaries:

_____
_____
_____
_____
_____
_____
_____
_____

Memories of Anniversaries:

_____
_____
_____
_____
_____
_____
_____
_____
_____
_____

Memories of Anniversaries:

_____
_____
_____
_____
_____
_____
_____
_____

Memories of Anniversaries:

_____
_____
_____
_____
_____
_____
_____
_____
_____

Memories of Anniversaries:

_____
_____
_____
_____
_____
_____
_____
_____

Section Six

Our Vacations & Adventures

I'm so glad I found you...

Our Vacations:

Date of trip/Location/ who we traveled with:
_____
_____
_____

One of our favorite memories:
_____
_____
_____
_____
_____

Date of trip/Location/ who we traveled with:
_____
_____
_____

One of our favorite memories:
_____
_____
_____
_____
_____

Our Vacations:

Date of trip/Location/ who we traveled with:
_____
_____
_____

One of our favorite memories:
_____
_____
_____
_____
_____

Date of trip/Location/ who we traveled with:
_____
_____
_____

One of our favorite memories:
_____
_____
_____
_____
_____

Our Vacations:

Date of trip/Location/who we traveled with:
_____
_____
_____

One of our favorite memories:
_____
_____
_____
_____

Date of trip/Location/who we traveled with:
_____
_____
_____

One of our favorite memories:
_____
_____
_____
_____

Our Vacations:

Date of trip/Location/who we traveled with:
_____
_____
_____

One of our favorite memories:
_____
_____
_____
_____

Date of trip/Location/who we traveled with:
_____
_____
_____

One of our favorite memories:
_____
_____
_____
_____

Our Vacations:

Date of trip/Location/who we traveled with:
_____
_____
_____

One of our favorite memories:
_____
_____
_____
_____

Date of trip/Location/who we traveled with:
_____
_____
_____

One of our favorite memories:
_____
_____
_____
_____

Our Vacations:

Date of trip / Location / who we traveled with:
_____
_____
_____

One of our favorite memories:
_____
_____
_____
_____

Date of trip / Location / who we traveled with:
_____
_____
_____

One of our favorite memories:
_____
_____
_____
_____

Our Vacations:

Date of trip/Location/who we traveled with:
_____
_____
_____

One of our favorite memories:
_____
_____
_____
_____

Date of trip/Location/who we traveled with:
_____
_____
_____

One of our favorite memories:
_____
_____
_____
_____

Our Vacations:

Date of trip/Location/who we traveled with:
_____
_____
_____

One of our favorite memories:
_____
_____
_____
_____

Date of trip/Location/who we traveled with:
_____
_____
_____

One of our favorite memories:
_____
_____
_____
_____

Our Vacations:

Date of trip/Location/ who we traveled with:
_____
_____
_____

One of our favorite memories:
_____
_____
_____
_____

Date of trip/Location/ who we traveled with:
_____
_____
_____

One of our favorite memories:
_____
_____
_____
_____

Our Vacations:

Date of trip/Location/ who we traveled with:
_____
_____

One of our favorite memories:
_____
_____
_____
_____

Date of trip/Location/ who we traveled with:
_____
_____

One of our favorite memories:
_____
_____
_____
_____

Section Seven

The Story Of Us

Here's to our happily ever after...

The Story of Us:

_____   _____
_____   _____
_____   _____
_____   _____
_____   _____
_____   _____
_____   _____
_____   _____
_____   _____
_____   _____

The Story of Us:

The Story of Us:

The Story of Us:

_____ _____
_____ _____
_____ _____
_____ _____
_____ _____
_____ _____
_____ _____
_____ _____

The Story of Us:

_____ _____
_____ _____
_____ _____
_____ _____
_____ _____
_____ _____
_____ _____
_____ _____
_____ _____

The Story of Us:

_____   _____
_____   _____
_____   _____
_____   _____
_____   _____
_____   _____
_____   _____
_____   _____

The Story of Us:

_____ _____
_____ _____
_____ _____
_____ _____
_____ _____
_____ _____
_____ _____
_____ _____

The Story of Us:

_____ _____
_____ _____
_____ _____
_____ _____
_____ _____
_____ _____
_____ _____
_____ _____

When I saw you I fell in love and you

smiled because you knew it.

-William Shakespeare

And they lived happily ever after..

www.ingramcontent.com/pod-product-compliance
Lightning Source LLC
Chambersburg PA
CBHW060503240426
43661CB00007B/901